A FLIP-THE-FLAP BOOK OF WILD ANIMALS

BEARS DON'T BOUNCE!

Jackie French
illustrated by Matt Cosgrove

BACKPACKBOOKS
o
NEW YORK

Text copyright © 2003 by Jackie French
Illustrations copyright © 2003 by Matt Cosgrove
This 2006 edition published by Backpack Books, New York, NY,
by arrangement with Allied Publishing Group, Inc.
All rights reserved.
ISBN 0-7607-7058-1
Manufactured in China
06 07 08 09 10 MCH 10 9 8 7 6 5 4 3 2 1
First US edition published in 2003 by Flying Frog Publishing,
an imprint of Allied Publishing Group, Inc.

Elephants don't

swing...

Kangaroos
don't surf...

Whales don't kiss...

Giraffes don't **jiggle...**

Penguins
don't prance...

Bears don't
bounce...

ZZZZZZZZZZZZZ...

all winter.

I'm not a bear...

but I love to sleep too.
Good night.